Law, Justice and Mediation

THE LEGEND OF SAINT YVES

Law, Justice and Mediation
The Legend of Saint Yves

Colour image edition. First edition published 2008.

Published 2014 by
WATERSIDE PRESS
Sherfield Gables
Sherfield on Loddon Hook
Hampshire RG27 0JG
United Kingdom

Telephone (+44) (0)1256 882250
E-mail enquiries@watersidepress.co.uk
Online catalogue and bookstore www.WatersidePress.co.uk

Copyright © 2008 and 2014 Bryan Gibson. All rights are hereby asserted and reserved by the author in accordance with UK and international law. No part of this book may be copied, reproduced, stored in any retrieval system or transmitted in any form or by any means, including in hard copy, electronically and via the internet, without the prior permission of Waterside Press to whom copyright has been assigned for the purposes of publication of this work worldwide.

Foreword ©2008 Marcel Berlins subject to the like terms and conditions.

Images All photographs © Waterside Press 2008.

ISBN 978 1 909976 06 1.

Cataloguing-In-Publication Data A catalogue record for this book can be obtained from the British Library.

Cover design © 2014 Waterside Press. Cover photograph of a wood carving in Quimper Cathedral of Saint Yves seated between a rich man and a poor man.

North American distributor Ingram Book Company, One Ingram Blvd, La Vergne, TN 37086, USA. Tel: (+1) 615 793 5000; inquiry@ingramcontent.com

Law, Justice and Mediation

THE LEGEND OF SAINT YVES

Bryan Gibson

With a Foreword by **Marcel Berlins**

≋ WATERSIDE PRESS

Acknowledgements

I am particularly grateful to Alex Gibson, Jane Green (Waterside Press House Editor) and Peter Williams for their various input, help and comments during the preparation of this book.

My special thanks are also due to Marcel Berlins for agreeing to write the *Foreword*. His regular articles for *The Guardian* frequently encapsulate values of the kind noted in this book and from time-to-time they provide a 'French connection' for practitioners, students and other readers to transport them beyond the realms of their everyday experience.

Bryan Gibson

January 2008

Law, Justice and Mediation
The Legend of Saint Yves

CONTENTS

Acknowledgements	iv
About the author	vi
Foreword by Marcel Berlins	vii
Dedication	ix
List of illustrations	xii
Introduction	15

CHAPTER

1.	The Legend of Saint Yves	19
2.	Not So Humble Origins	29
3.	Don't Forget the Poor	37
4.	Mediator, Counsellor, Lawyer, Judge	47
5.	Miracle Worker	55
6.	Tributes by the Score	63
	Epilogue	73
	Appendix: Extract from *The Golden Legend*	81
	Index	91

About the author

Bryan Gibson grew up in South Yorkshire before moving to Cambridge, Salisbury, Bristol, London, Basingstoke and Winchester during his legal career. He is a barrister, former co-editor of *Justice of the Peace* and a regular contributor to that journal and other media. He founded Waterside Press in 1989 and has since written, edited and published a wide range of books on aspects of crime and punishment whilst compiling an *A-Z of Criminal Justice* (forthcoming).

The author of the Foreword

Marcel Berlins is a writer, journalist, broadcaster and university lecturer. Educated in South Africa, France and Britain (London School of Economics), he has been legal correspondent of *The Times*, a regular *Guardian* columnist since 1988, and was for many years presenter of BBC Radio 4's 'Law in Action'. He has written, co-written or edited several books on legal themes.

Foreword

A few years ago—I've forgotten in what context—I happened to mention in an article I'd written that lawyers had a patron saint, and that he was St Yves, a Frenchman. Most readers who commented—including many English lawyers—admitted ignorance of this fact and expressed surprise. They asked me questions about him, which I could not answer—my ignorance was only slightly less than theirs. I remember one cynical remark in particular: 'I suppose he's also the patron saint of greed and lying'. That says a lot for common attitudes today, but it was also true of the 13th century, when a serious young man called Erwan Helouri, from Tréguier in Brittany, followed his religious studies with Thomas Aquinas by becoming an advocate.

Bryan Gibson has researched his life with passion and enthusiasm and emerges with a fascinating portrayal of the man behind the sainthood. In a society rife with corrupt and bribable lawyers, where only the well-off could afford to pay for legal services, Helouri acted for the poor and vulnerable, often for nothing. He campaigned for the law to be simpler to understand and more accessible. Later, as a parish priest, he was a pioneer of what we now call mediation. His preoccupations were no different from those we still consider important today.

Calling St. Yves the patron saint of lawyers, Bryan Gibson argues, is misleading. It suggests that lawyers pray to him when they desire a rich client, a financially rewarding trial, an undeserved judicial decision or wrongful acquittal. It may be that lawyers do pray for these things and perhaps, occasionally, St Yves obliges. But it would be more accurate, if less pithy, if he were to be known as the patron saint of justice, of the law's fairness and its compassion.

Whether or not you believe he performed the miracles for which he was sanctified does not matter. What is important is that he was clearly a good man, worthy of the adoration and respect he's been receiving over seven centuries in places where people do know of his story. St Yves deserves to be far better known than he is, especially in the English-speaking world, and in Bryan Gibson he has found a worthy champion.

Marcel Berlins January 2008

Dedication

To Kara, Alex and Verity

With fond memories of our holidays in France and other places

The cloisters at Tréguier Cathedral date from the 15th century.

List of illustrations

The cloisters at Tréguier Cathedral date from the 15th century xi

Immaculately kept civic buildings at Tréguier 18

Statue of St Yves in the nave of Tréguier Cathedral 24

Food in abundance: the lid of a sardine tin 28

The cover of a children's book 34

Close-up of a placard 36

The well-worn poor box at Tréguier 39

A representative of the poor on the cathedral steps 40

The noticeably up-market St Yves Gallery 42

The rich man's bag of gold 44

St Yves between a rich man and a poor man in Quimper Cathedral 46

Confessional booths in Tréguier Cathedral 50

A woman holding up her child for a blessing 52

The tomb of St Yves 54

Statuette of St Yves by a sailing boat 59

A Breton half-timbered house 60

St Yves in close-up 62

The fretwork spire of Tréguier Cathedral 66

St Yves between a rich man and a poor man in Tréguier Cathedral 72

Facing East: a stained glass window depicts the two local saints 74

St Tudual, or Tudwall, or Tugdall 75

The author scrutinises another source 77

All photographs © Waterside Press.

Introduction

Introduction

I first visited Brittany in north-west France over 25 years ago, chancing upon the small fishing port-cum-market town of Tréguier. More to the point, that is how I came to visit its magnificent Gothic cathedral and encounter Erwan Helouri, later St Yves.[1] On my return, I wrote a piece for the weekly courts newspaper, *Justice of the Peace*, charting the life and times of an individual whom I deemed to be a giant of law, justice, counselling and mediation. Outside of Brittany and in a pre-internet age, I could find few, if any, references to him.

This book was prompted by a return visit to Tréguier in the summer of 2007 and is an attempt to draw the legend of St Yves to wider notice. It concerns a defender of the poor in the face of power and influence, a person of unusual wisdom who was also an early advocate of what we would now call human rights and restorative justice. Like all legends and folk tales, that of St Yves has been embroidered across the years—as have those of Robin Hood, Jesse James or Pretty Boy Floyd stealing from the rich to help the poor. All rely on enduring notions of 'true', 'moral' or 'poetic' justice, despite their different cultural backdrops and associations. It is refreshing that both Robin Hood and St Yves can be traced back to the same broad timeframe of the 12th and 13th centuries, which may be indicative of a yet earlier and more universal tradition of handing down stories of hope and encouragement.

There is an inescapable religious context to what follows, but this is not intended as a spiritual tract. Neither is it anything to do with Roman Catholic proliferation of sainthood (see *Chapter 1*), although it is understandable that the story never made any great impact within what was subsequently a guardedly Protestant Britain. With the social turmoil of the French Revolution and fear of such developments spreading, the door was perhaps even more firmly closed (though, ironically, St Yves' tomb was wrecked in the aftermath of those events). Rather, it is the story that counts, not its ecclesiastical or biblical traces. I do not doubt that it has its equivalents in Muslim, Hindu and Pagan circles. Within an increasingly global context I would like to think that the legend of St Yves is part of some common heritage in which hope is kept alive by stories in which truth and justice prevail.

---

[1] Or 'St Yvo' as noted in the text.

In contrast, I remain sceptical if open-minded about the miracles described in *Chapter 5* (I have, for example, come across a number of lawyers with a reputation for being able to appear in two places at once!) and touched by, yet uncertain about, the countless tributes of those people who claim to have benefitted from St Yves' largesse as described in *Chapter 6*. But credit where it is due. None of these events would have been possible but for the earlier, pioneering work of a Welsh monk, St Tugdual, who founded the first monastery at Tréguier as noted in the *Epilogue*.

Saint Yves is commonly described as 'the patron saint of lawyers'—but as I suggest in the text (and whatever The Vatican may assert) this can be misleading. Closer examination shows that his reputation was based on broader and more substantial foundations—those of justice, fairness and an ability to mediate between or assist people in intractable situations. I have thus taken the liberty of shifting the emphasis. Similarly, it can be noted that what Robin Hood (and comparable 'local heroes' the world over) achieved with slings, arrows, crossbows or six-guns, St Yves achieved via reasoned argument, debate, explanation and consensus.

Little had changed by the time of my return to Tréguier in 2007 other than my own perceptions. Tributes were still being laid at the tomb of St Yves, the same images, effigies and statues remained on display (the cobwebs were new, I guess), the poor box still hung from the wall of the civic offices and, as ever, a representative of those whom St Yves sought to help had positioned himself strategically on the cathedral steps to plead for eurocents. Unlike last time, there was no offending Rolls Royce in the cathedral car park but there was a spanking new Bentley cabriolet with a personalised registration plate. St Yves would have appreciated the juxtaposition. It was just as difficult to unearth hard facts – and, again, I had missed the one day of the year when the 'reliquary' of the saint (a casket containing his bones and effects) is paraded through the town.

An outsider of sorts, St Yves was no outcast or misfit even if some of those he represented fell under that umbrella as described in *Chapter 3*. He worked from within the established order, winning the admiration of people of diverse backgrounds and points of view. But he stood up to be counted and for values of decency, integrity and equilibrium. In short, the legend of St Yves may give sustenance to those judges, lawyers, mediators, counsellors and students of human nature who believe that justice is better served by striving to make a difference and keeping conflict at bay.

CHAPTER 1

The Legend of St Yves

Immaculately kept civic buildings at Tréguier.

CHAPTER 1

The Legend of St Yves

It is always fascinating to discover a new interest. That is how I felt about the life and work of Erwan Helouri, also known as Yvo Héloury, later St Yves. It was strange that I had not heard of him before. Even now, 25 years on, I have seen only the briefest of references to him except in specialist works. Yet his story is of great import to anyone involved with crime and punishment, or, indeed, resolving conflict of any kind. It is about how—in an age of bribery and corruption—a young man from a small town in France rose to become a touchstone for truth, fairness and justice. I hope that other people will find the legend of St Yves and its background equally stimulating and thought provoking.

IN SEARCH OF ST YVES

People involved with the administration of justice in Britain, the USA or other English-speaking countries might be forgiven for not pricking-up their ears when the name St Yves is mentioned. Sometimes called St Yvo[1] and described as the patron saint of lawyers, he has no great profile in those parts of the world. No emblems on legal stationery, no St Yves paperweights, no rings, medallions, symbols or motifs. Neither does he figure prominently in encyclopaedias, libraries or collections.[2] His single-handed fight against prejudice, discrimination, bigotry and intolerance goes equally uncharted. Yet, from a time when the monarch was all-powerful—and wealth and influence all-pervading—he has a claim to fame as valid as that of Robin Hood, Jessie James, Ned Kelly and individuals of similar ilk.

Champion of the poor
Like those other folk heroes, St Yves was a champion of the poor and disinherited, someone for whom no cause was too marginal or likely to

---

[1] Especially in France. For a short note on the quite different 'St Ives' of Cornwall and Cambridgeshire, UK, see the *Epilogue*.
[2] So far as I know, there is no (previous) book in English about his life and work.

be shirked due to its unpopularity. His reputation was founded on an ability to redress the balance between rich and poor—at least in the immediate sense—especially if this meant publicly shaming the better-off into the bargain. His popularity was enhanced by the ingenuity with which he was able to do this, causing many of the tales about him to take on a mythical quality. The belief was that he would never let the underdog down and would materialise, in body or in spirit, whenever he might be needed.

An age of corruption

The charming Episcopal market town-cum-fishing haven of Tréguier lies some 50 kilometres west of St Malo on what is a lesser road between Paimpol and Lannion. Despite its modest size and out-of-the-way location, Tréguier possesses a magnificent Gothic cathedral. There, shielded from the mid-day sun and no doubt somewhat mesmerised by the grandeur of the surroundings, is where I first heard the story that forms the central part of this book. On my return home I decided to find out more. Those early researches led to an article which was published in the courts newspaper, *Justice of the Peace,* announcing the existence of a hitherto (so it seemed) unsung hero of law, justice, counselling and mediation.

A somewhat flimsy *Dictionary of Saints* which I happened upon contained the following rudimentary information:

> **St Ivo** ... judge of the Rennes diocesan court ... 'the poor man's advocate' ... mediator ... *the* patron saint of lawyers.

The tourist guides were and are more forthcoming. For example, the Automobile Association's *Explorer Britanny,*[3] in a section headed 'Land of Saints', reads as follows:

> **Yves Helouri** (1253-1303) was born in Minihy-Tréguier.[4] The patron saint of lawyers, Yves combined religious duties with his work as a magistrate and advocate in Tréguier, and was famously incorruptible in an age when most lawyers took bribes. He was a champion of the poor, and is often depicted standing between a well-dressed client and a man in rags ...

---

[3] 1999 (onwards), Hunt, Lindsay, Automobile Association.
[4] Or, to be yet more precise, Kermartin, a hamlet nearby.

That entry continues by summarising one of the most famous stories about St Yves:

> A rich man sued a beggar for loitering by his kitchen door and 'stealing' his cooking smells. St Yves heard the evidence, declared that the rich man had won his case, and awarded him appropriate damages—the sound of a coin rattling in a tin!

This and similarly iconic tales are a recurring feature of the legend. In amongst references to St Yves' aesthetic life, death at the age of 49, marble encased tomb in Tréguier Cathedral and snapshots from his early life, other guides contain a patchwork of information concerning his career and miracles. Always, with varying degrees of embellishment, these are accompanied by some assertion along the lines: 'He received the poor man's petition, but refused the rich man's purse'. Yet, outside of Brittany and in a pre-internet age, I could find few solid references to the events described in the following chapters. Indeed, it was a children's book complete with speech bubbles and idealised images that first put me on the trail of the larger picture—and, eventually, *The Golden Legend* described in *Chapter 5*, extracts from which I have included in an appendix.

Myth, fable and hard evidence
As with many legends, no doubt much will have changed in the telling and re-telling. In St Yves' case, translation first from the Latin, the only written language of his own time, into Breton, then French, and finally English is bound to have led to the kind of discrepancies inherent in such processes. Then there are questions about how well things carry over time, the reliability of the original witnesses who gave evidence to a Papal Enquiry that lasted for several years during the 1330s and the paraphernalia, rituals and euphoria that have sprung up in more modern times in support of the legend that will have served to bolster a certain understanding of events. Some re-assessment and critique may thus be appropriate at a later stage.

SAINTS FOR ALL SEASONS

There are, I have learned, saints for virtually every occasion, event and group of people (and animals and inanimate objects) under the sun. There are saints for everyone from pregnant women to speleologists (people concerned with the science of caves) and explosives workers, from fishermen to brewers—who qualify for no less than three! There are saints of tax collectors, people who have been poisoned and those suffering from toothache. Brittany itself is over run with saints, popular wisdom having it that there are 'seven thousand, seven hundred and seven score and seven'.[5]

Examples of sainthood
In the context of crime and punishment alone, there is a saint of jurists (St John of Capistrano); one for policemen (St Michael); one for social workers (St Louise de Marrilac); four for prisoners (including St Barbara and St Dismas[6]—the 'good thief' who, according to the *New Testament*, was crucified alongside Jesus Christ); and a quite distinct saint for the prison itself (St Joseph). It must also be a comfort to the 'falsely accused' to know that not only do they have the Court of Appeal and the Criminal Cases Review Commission to safeguard their interests, but heavenly guardians in the shape of St Raymond (Nonnatus) and St Dominic Savio.

This tendency to place matters in neat pigeon-holes may have done St Yves a disservice—as I will urge in later chapters—since his attributes seem to go far wider than those of any lawyer or judge in that capacity alone. Further to this, my experience of legal gatherings (albeit in the UK) suggests that St Yves goes unrecognised and is perhaps best described as anonymous. I have never witnessed a toast being drunk nor a vote of thanks cast to his memory. Maybe it is different in France where even ordinary citizens show overwhelming gratitude: *Chapter 6*.

Other contenders
Only St Yves is generally claimed as *the* patron saint of lawyers and to occupy that role internationally (or even globally: despite the somewhat parochial nature of his travels and activities as noted in *Chapters 2* and *4*). However, it seems right to acknowledge two other leading contenders, St Genesius and St Thomas More.[7]

---

[5] I make this 7,847.
[6] Hence 'Fragments of a Deposition of Christ: The Good Thief' a painting by Perino del Vaga, acquired by Charles I and still part of the Royal Collection; and The Society of St Dismus, a charity for ex-prisoners in Southampton.
[7] Others include St Mark and St Raymond of Penyafort.

St Genesius
St Genesius, who died at around the start of the 4th century, was what in modern times would have been described as a lawyers' clerk or, in more up-to-date terms, a legal executive.[8] But he is also sometimes described as a notary, which in some countries is a synonym for lawyer. Like Asterix, the indomitable French comic book character, St Genesius hailed from Gaul, and is often described as 'a servant of the court'. When the Emperors Diocletian and Maximian ordered the persecution of Christians, Genesius, to his eternal credit, refused to recognise their decrees. He was singled out as a trouble-maker, forced to become a fugitive and was captured and beheaded on the bank of the River Rhône.

St Thomas More
The other chief contender is the Englishman St Thomas More (1478-1535)—a statesman and dissident who was also beheaded. He studied law at the Inns of Court in London and was called to the bar by Lincoln's Inn in 1501. He was appointed Lord Chancellor in 1529, only to fall from favour under Henry VIII, including for his 'treasonable silence' in refusing to comment on the Act of Supremacy. Thomas More is known for actions beyond those that relate to his professional background and is thus perhaps best treated as a saint who happened to be a lawyer.

Keeping his head
St Yves did not lose his head; rather his reputation rests on his keeping it when people all about him were finding life difficult. Without knowing anything of the finer points of the arrangements for saintly elevation, which it is to be hoped are unimpeachable, it is possible to venture that it appears to be a regular feature that the subject will, at some point, have stepped out of line, challenged or been in conflict with authority, the latter often being cast, with hindsight, in the role of the oppressor. In one atypical situation, Erwan Helouri 'relieved' King Philippe III's generals of property looted from Tréguier (a matter of only marginal weight in the decision to make him a saint). But normally he does not appear to have acted radically by engaging skirmishes with the powers that be. He challenged the status quo more by 'shining example' than direct action.

---

[8] Perhaps he should be adopted for that specific role. He is sometimes styled the patron saint of actors, dancers, clowns, attorneys and victims of torture!

Statue of St Yves in the nave of Tréguier Cathedral.

Saintly protocol
Given that there are innumerable saints (especially in Brittany: see above), they must share their annual day with other incumbents, as St Yves does with St Ciarán, St Emeliana, St Pudentia, St Theophilus and others. But his own festival, held on the closest Sunday to May 19—and known as the Pardon of St Yves—would seem to far outshine those of his peers. This is the day on which upwards of 10,000 lawyers and other pilgrims congregate in Tréguier for the weekend to seek forgiveness (i.e. 'pardon') for the sins that they have committed during and maybe throughout the year!

Yet St Yves might still disappear without trace in Brittany with its seven thousand, seven score, etc. saints. But many of those saints only aspire to the lower rungs of sainthood—what is sometimes called 'local sainthood'—and they go unrecognised except by custom, tradition and usage. In contrast, St Yves is what might be described as a fully accredited saint. Another pointer to his high status is the fact that he was canonised just 44 years after his death. He transcends popular culture and mythology, and in France stands shoulder-to-shoulder with such notables as Joan of Arc and Bernadette of Lourdes.

ORIGINS OF THE LEGEND

If Brittany is a place of saints, it is also a land of ghosts, intrigue and mystery. It is where, in the Paimpol Forest, the Knights of the Round Table first set out on their quest for the Holy Grail. It is the home of Merlin and other makers of magic. There is a powerful culture of folk tales such as that in many Celtic parts of Britain and Ireland or remoter regions such as Cornwall or parts of Wales. In parts of Brittany there are traces of earlier civilizations evidenced by monolithic riddles that challenge Stonehenge with their claim to world heritage status. It is a heady mix.

A place of ghosts, myths and superstition
There are also ghosts of a more recent variety, Brittany having lost more of its population per head in the First World War than any other part of Europe, and on either side in that conflict. Reputedly, there was a time when menfolk were so scarce that the survival of the region was at stake, with mass migration to the cities an added complication in terms of

keeping up the land. It is also for longstanding historical reasons a place of separatism, if not naturally radical or given to uprisings. Even today the Black and White flag of Brittany is proudly displayed by people who, like many people in Wales, Scotland or, say, the Basque region of Spain, regard themselves as naturally apart. It is also a place of contradictions: where the *Bonnets Rouges* (Red Caps) rampaged against the unbridled taxation of the Sun King, Louis XIV and yet the *Association Breton* (or Chouans), remnants of the aristocracy, banded together with other local people against the 'Godless excesses' of the revolutionaries of 1789. It is where the French underground acted in secretive ways to create and support Allied escape routes in the Second World War.[9] It is a place with ample reasons for its people to seek out some bridge between the here and now and whatever may follow, whilst its mystique, sometimes faded elegance and history of reprisals, counter-reprisals and atrocities is all part of this same backdrop.

Witnesses and evidence

St Yves has been a favourite son of the Bretons since his own time and his remembrance pervades the town of Tréguier especially. But he is also to be encountered elsewhere. I came across his effigy in Quimper to the west and in the porch of the church at Belle Isle, the tiny and isolated offshore island a couple of hours sailing time from the historic naval port of Quiberon. There, the rich man's bag of gold was even more in evidence, virtually thrust into the hands of the visitor as a form of temptation as he or she enters the building.

The story of St Yves is frequently told in flashback, via the accounts of the 200 or so ageing witnesses who assembled in Tréguier from 1330 onwards to relate matters to the Papal Enquiry. That enquiry scrutinised every corner of the subject's life, every known day of it, right back to the time of his birth. Each witness was then cross-examined concerning his or her personal experiences of Erwan Helouri. Two bishops and an abbot listened on 23 separate days spread over several years to the life of the child, boy, youth, student, lawyer, judge, priest and miracle worker before reporting their findings to The Vatican. What follows is based in part upon what those witnesses told the enquiry as it has been handed down through the generations.

---

[9] It is also, in passing, where Jules Verne, author of *Twenty Thousand Leagues Under the Sea,* and other works came from.

CHAPTER 2

Not So Humble Origins

Food in abundance: the lid of a sardine tin decorated with a view of Tréguier Cathedral cloisters. Whole stores are given over to the humble sardine right across Brittany. Excellent and plentiful, they were once a staple diet of the poor. There is a certain irony in their modern-day elevation to the delicatessen counter.

CHAPTER 2

Not So Humble Origins

The witnesses to the Papal Enquiry of the 1330s described how Erwan Helouri's life was lived in austerity and piety. He would always give to other people the benefit of those unsought advantages that might have been 'forced upon him' through the circumstances of his own birth and later station in life. The witnesses deposed as to how he would give away his possessions, offer accommodation to those without shelter and generally help and support anyone in need.

Open door policy
His open door policy was both symbolic and real. It extended to the physical removal of doors and window shutters. He argued that anyone who needed justice should be able to see at once that nothing stood in its way, regardless of their origins or status in life. Everyone should have access to justice and be free to seek it.

The witnesses also described how, in later life, Erwan Helouri founded a free hospital and laid the foundations for the present-day cathedral. With renovations, that cathedral still stands, more or less in its original form (but with various additions), despite the fact that the ornate windows and many of the furnishings were destroyed in the French Revolution (*Chapter 6*).

Some people may think that 'as a story' it is disappointing to learn that Erwan Helouri started out in life from a position of comparative privilege. Some versions of his life downplay this aspect and describe him as coming from more humble origins. Others point out that although his father owned an estate theirs was not the most prestigious of manor houses! Most versions of his life seek to identify some trigger from the past that places him firmly on the side of those less fortunate than himself.

EARLY LIFE AND CAREER

Erwan Helouri was born in Kermartin, Minihy-Tréguier, about two kilometres from Tréguier itself. He was the son of noble and well-to-do parents—what might equate nowadays to being middle-class or even upper middle-class (to the extent that such descriptions still have currency). As a child, he learned to read, write and appreciate the fine arts through the home tuition of his educated mother. His father, who had served in The Crusades with 'Good King Louis IX' (St Louis), insisted that the young Erwan—his Christian name being used by all, even after he became a judge!—not only master the standard country and combative pursuits of riding, hunting and handling a sword, but also that he work for long hours in the fields with the local peasants 'in order to experience life at first hand'. This seems to have been regarded by many witnesses as part of the underpinning for his later actions, pragmatism and common touch.

Further education

At the age of 14, Erwan was sent to Paris to study philosophy, theology and canon law at the university there. He was accompanied by his lifelong friend and confidant, Jehan.[1] Apart from missing his Breton box-bed—'Yet it is so marvellous to have the chance to understand the ways of different people'—Erwan appears to have been oblivious to the hardships of student life in what is now the Latin Quarter. He is frequently depicted as hard-working, studious, religiously inclined and dismissive of the usual distractions of time at university. Reportedly, he was a model student, if somewhat reckless with his own welfare, finding little time for meals, sleep or entertainment, so engrossed did he become in his studies. On top of this, fasting was to become a regular feature of his regular routine in later life, particularly if this allowed some poor person to eat his share.

St Thomas Aquinas

The eager-to-learn Erwan was doubly fortunate in his tutor, arguably amongst the finest that any budding theologian might wish for, in the Italian scholar Thomas Aquinas (1225-1274)—later St Thomas, the patron saint of universities and colleges—regarded by many observers as the most towering intellect in the Roman Catholic Church. According to the *Encyclopaedia Britannica*, St Thomas Aquinas was a Christian philosopher who developed his own conclusions starting from the premises of Aristotle, notably 'in the metaphysics of personality, creation, and Providence'. As a

---

[1] Who appears to have benefited from a cost-free, vicarious scholarship.

theologian he was responsible in two masterworks, the *Summa Theologiae* and the *Summa Contra Gentiles*, for the classical systematisation of Latin theology. He was also a poet who wrote 'some of the most gravely beautiful eucharistic hymns in the church's liturgy'. He was placed in a monastery as a child, where he grew up, but then became caught up in the mass expulsion of monks under Emperor Frederick II. Caught between the vicissitudes of family preoccupations and state manipulation he found liberation at the University of Naples before joining a group of mendicant friars, the Dominicans, who forsook worldly values to live in poverty:

> Normally, his work is presented as the integration into Christian thought of the recently rediscovered Aristotelian philosophy, in competition with the integration of Platonic thought effected by the Fathers of the Church during the first 12 centuries of the Christian Era. This view is essentially correct; more radically, however, it should also be asserted that Thomas' work accomplished an evangelical awakening to the need for a cultural and spiritual renewal not only in the lives of individual men but also throughout the church. Thomas must be understood in his context as a mendicant religious, influenced both by the evangelism of St. Francis of Assisi, founder of the Franciscan order, and by the devotion to scholarship of St. Dominic, founder of the Dominican order.

Here then, it is possible to glean some idea as to how the influence of Thomas Aquinas would have been superimposed on those values already inherited by Erwan Helouri from his days in the fields—all, at a time of upheaval, argument, debate and change in both Western and Arab worlds, such that there was a need for people who were prepared to strike out in new directions whilst standing up for decency, fair treatment and the rejection of purely worldly values. Erwan's hours of study were further enhanced by boundless insomnia and unchecked energy.

The first miracle and a masters' degree

When money was short, Erwan had a ready answer, often quoted as being his first miracle (see further *Chapter 5*). He sat down on a street corner with his bagpipes (the traditional Breton instrument) and, within an hour, the streets would be awash with singing and dancing and his upturned hat on the pavement brimming with coins. The stories describe him as promptly making over his earnings to Jehan, who would feed both themselves and the needy. This seemingly inherent ability to obtain the wherewithal to continue his life's work is a recurring motif.

At age 20, Erwan took a Master of Arts degree in theology, having excelled also at Latin, science and philosophy. It is said that he was offered a chair by Paris University but turned it down so that he could concentrate on more important matters.

DESTINY IN THE TWINKLING OF AN EYE

The scenario now and as told in the children's books switches to sparsely furnished lodgings where two post-graduate students are passing the small hours pondering on the meaning and purpose of life. Whilst looking for direction, Erwan suddenly comes out with an all-important question which is to shape his destiny:

'Jehan, what do you know of the law?'

Following an evasive response—Jehan is frequently cast as the stooge at key moments—Erwan explains to his bemused friend that ordinary and untrained people need lawyers to guide them through the difficulties created by the law itself. The following words, part of the legend, now adorn the wall of many a French lawyer's room:

> The law is so complicated that people cannot understand it. Help me find a way to deny its weaknesses.[2]

Learning the law
With what is by now infectious enthusiasm, the pair set out the very next morning for Orléans to study civil law there under the tutelage of the celebrated jurist Peter de la Chapelle. So commences a span of some ten years, during which Erwan Helouri grapples with the intricacies of his new-found vocation. Yet he is not without self-doubt. There is an inner conflict: whether to serve the church or the law? Fortuitously and almost

---

[2] Translated but remaining as true to the original as possible. Here, of course, lies the rub, since many people would say that it is lawyers and law-makers who contribute most to that complexity!

magically the dilemma is resolved for him. At the conclusion of his studies, Erwan is offered a post which combines elements of both. At the age of just 29, he is appointed as the diocesan judge—or magistrate, the terms are used indiscriminately; in substance he takes sole charge of law and order in the area—in one of the largest cities in the region, Rennes. It is an appointment which carries a high degree of status and he moves into a luxuriously appointed apartment in the Bishop's Palace.

It is, at least temporarily, a case of *'Au revoir, Jehan'* as Erwan sets out for the first time on a life of his own. The story of his active involvement and development as a counsellor, mediator, lawyer and judge is told in *Chapter 4*. It sometimes describes an ideal world in which judgement and decision-making are unclouded by irrelevant or extraneous considerations and guided by the surest rules and touch.

The front cover of a book for children. In the mythology, St Yves is usually portrayed as being of a wholly gentle nature, with blue eyes and flaxen hair. In a recurring motif, a woman offers up her child to be blessed, whilst the sick and the lame wait in the hope of a cure. Even the dog in the foreground looks content. This work from the Paris-based publisher of Editions Fleurus depicts Erwan Helouri through the medium of the cartoon at his benevolent (sometimes dreamlike) best. Telling the story in an accessible way, it is a good starting point for any reader who has a basic understanding of the French language.

CHAPTER 3

Don't Forget the Poor

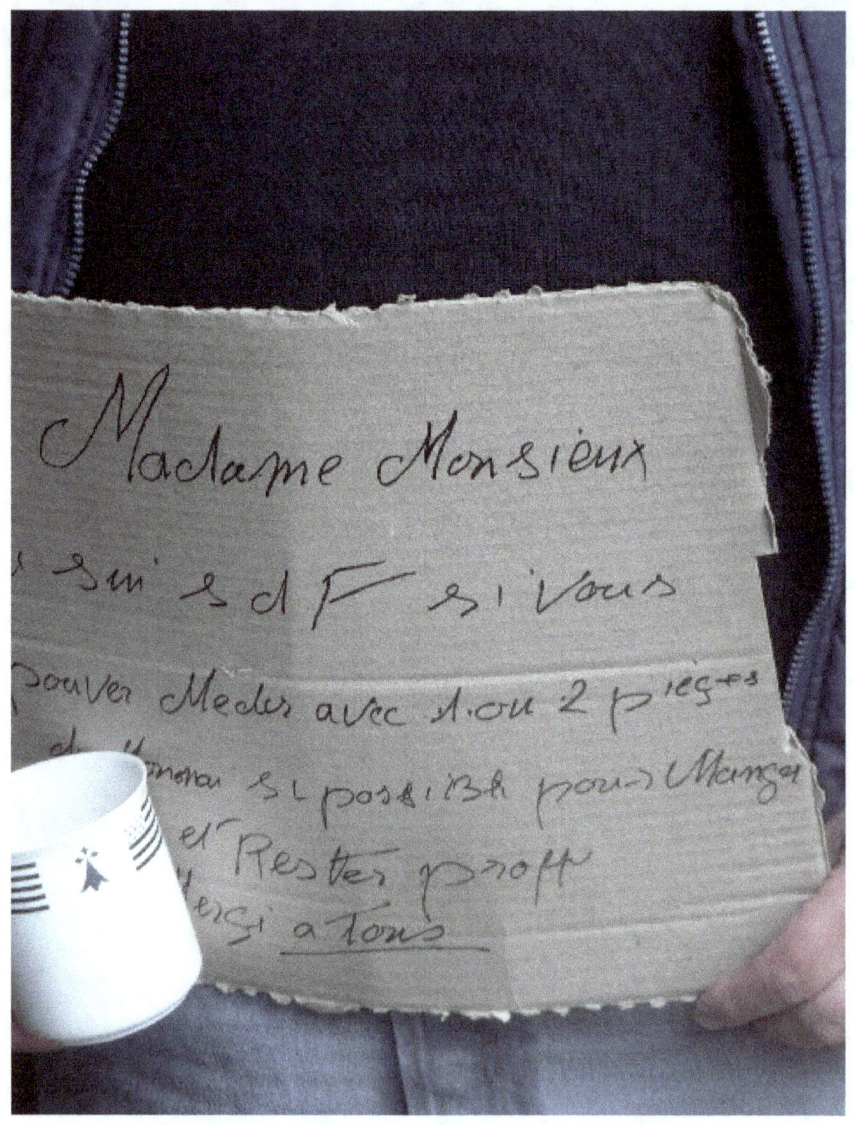

A beggar's placard. In short: 'Thanking you for small coins, so that I can eat and rest'.

CHAPTER 3

Don't Forget the Poor

There is a poor box in the Hotel de Ville at Tréguier. It has seen better days. It is well-worn and suitably distressed. Its tiny door swings open at the slightest touch. It is made of wood, oak probably. There is no money inside, whether 'small money'[1] or otherwise. It is an antique, for exhibition only, that stands alongside other historic items, something of a collectors' item, but doubly meaningful when on show in the place where the tensions between rich and poor were played out and passed into legend.[2]

The poor box acts as a reminder of the time when similar receptacles were in daily use in courthouses, police stations and in other public buildings around Britain. Even today, in some places, resort may be had to one, in reality or metaphorically speaking, when a hand-out is in order, but the world has moved on. Modern-day, western-style poverty is a relative concept unlike that in parts of the Third World. The poor box in Tréguier has a complementary wooden plaque above it, emblazoned with the words *N'oubliez pas des pauvres*—Don't forget the poor.

MISFITS, VAGABONDS AND NE'ER-DO-WELLS

As noted in *Chapter 2*, as a youth, Erwan Helouri was obliged to take his turn in the fields alongside local farm workers, as part of his education and upbringing. In later life he was to befriend countless misfits, vagabonds and people on the fringes of the community, mostly poor people or those unable to fend for themselves. His reputation is based on the fact that despite his elevation in the world he remembered and helped them. Having qualified as a lawyer, he recalled the complexities that the law creates for outsiders and began to speak up for them. Hence, he is variously described as 'the poor man's advocate', 'a champion of

---

[1] The use of this term is noted later in the chapter.
[2] It is not secured to the wall and goes unguarded, so that it is indeed surprising that no-one has 'collected it' before now.

the poor' and 'defender of the poor'. Here, 'poor' includes those forced into that state by circumstances: the sick, injured or lame at a time when there was no public safety-net and medical advice and medicines could be unusually expensive. He is credited with founding a Free Hospital at Tréguier, at a time when the word hospital was liberally construed to mean a place not just of healing but one where nourishment and sustenance might be provided.[3]

More mythical tales
Stories abound of Erwan Helouri's largesse. Thus, for example, witnesses who gave evidence to the Papal Enquiry of the 1330s told the assessors that when he was appointed as a judge, Erwan told the tailor who arrived to measure him for his flowing robes to forget his task and to donate the cloth and fur to needy children, who were more deserving of the warmth. He took in vagabonds at his quarters in the Bishop's Palace and shared his home, food and time with them. At one stage, so it was reported, he adopted two delinquent orphans. They were given a four-poster bed whilst he slept on the floor. Similar tales tell of him sleeping on a hurdle or doorstep to experience what real poverty means.

Festive occasions were marked by open invitations to the poor to visit him as part of the open door policy already noted in *Chapter 2*—and he welcomed gypsies, migrants and other people who lived on the margins of the community, especially those hounded by the authorities or branded by other people as ne'er-do-wells. There is a certain vibrancy in the images that have been created depicting those times. There are dangers in nostalgia and it is likely that those times were harder and perhaps less enjoyable than is sometimes portrayed. It is possible to forget about poverty for a while, but it is not solved without dealing with entrenched social structures and deep-rooted inequality. As with the miracles described in *Chapter 5* there is sometimes a sense that events may occasionally have been driven by euphoria, hysteria or been seen, with hindsight, through rose-tinted spectacles. The legend of St Yves draws attention to the condition of the poor and highlights their plight but does not offer any all-embracing solution or blueprint for change. Yet

---

[3] Examples of this kind of hospital can be found in the history of the UK, such as the Hospital of St Cross in Winchester, where travellers can still, today, knock on the door and request the freely available Wayfarers Dole of bread and ale.

the images are from a time when poverty was of a different order to that of today, when its very recognition may have been all-important.

The well-used (but now disused) poor box on display at the Hotel de Ville (town hall) in Tréguier. It is decorated with tall sunflowers, a staple crop of the region, and depicts a lamb guarded over by a sword that also forms the shape of a cross. I am told that the latter image signifies the *Agnus Dei* or 'Lamb of God'.

Modern-day ambassador of the poor, strategically positioned on the cathedral steps—delighted and proud to be photographed in return for some 'small money'. A character from life in a place where stories, illustration and artworks of the rich and poor occupy their own genre.

Of the many recurring images that accompany the legend of St Yves, one depicts him standing or sitting between two litigants, the first person in fine clothes, forcefully holding on to his bag of gold, the second in the tattered garments of a poor man or beggar. The latter sometimes clutches a nominal coin of base metal for all that he is worth. Variations on this theme show these two would-be litigants, manifestly from the extremes of the social spectrum, holding legal documents, scrolls or petitions. The image conveys more about the legend of St Yves and his understanding of the excesses of monetary-based social inequality than words ever can.

This same world of differences is mirrored in the events of the present-day, if maybe not so stark in their implications. On each of my visits to Tréguier a 'self-appointed representative' of the poor has been positioned on the cathedral steps asking for spare coins, or, in direct translation, 'small money' (which has a far more unspoiled ring to it!). In the Place de Matray directly opposite the north door of the cathedral there has been a young man with an emaciated-looking dog on a piece of string and a couple of down-and-outs (if not street drinkers) such as might be seen in many a town centre—and one, or sometimes a couple, of women looking pale, bedraggled and undernourished. This pageant is occasionally added to by other noticeably less-well-off people, heading for the tourist alleyways or street corners with their begging bowls, tins, Breton mugs, cardboard boxes or upturned collecting hats. They do not offer active entertainment in return as Erwan Helouri did on the streets of Paris (what a lawyer would term 'consideration') and neither are there signs—as, instantly, there were for the seemingly more fortunate Erwan—of manna from Heaven (see *Chapter 2*).

Yet all around there is evidence of wealth and a quite different lifestyle. This presents itself in the form of fine clothes, quality cars, superior hotels and restaurants and up-market boutiques. Just as I was struck by the magnificent confessional booths in the cathedral (a sign perhaps that this might be a place where a fair level of sin occurs and falls to be forgiven: see the pictures in *Chapter 5*), I could not help noticing on my first visit the Rolls Royce in the car park, just yards from the cathedral steps, that by my visit of 2007 had metamorphosed into a gleaming new Bentley Cabriolet. It is surreal and somewhat unnerving that this juxtaposition is but a stone's throw from St Yves' tomb. It heightens the sensitivities and brings home the legend with a most unusual impact.

The noticeably up-market St Yves Gallery with its stock of fine artworks and souvenirs. The gallery occupies one of the many attractive and well-preserved Breton-style buildings with their half-timbered upper floors.

THE RICH MAN AND THE POOR MAN

Just inside the huge wooden doors of Tréguier Cathedral, high on the stone wall, to the right, is an ancient wood-carving based upon a story that is integral to the legend of St Yves.

Écoute, ding, dong...
One day, a wealthy merchant brought a vagabond before Erwan Helouri when he was sitting as a judge in court. The claim was that each evening for the past week the vagabond had crept low along the wall and positioned himself directly beneath the kitchen window of the merchant's home to delight in the aromas from the succulent meats roasting over the huge fire within. The merchant asked that the vagabond be made to pay for that privilege, whilst the vagabond in turn relied upon the somewhat novel defence, 'I could not help myself, I just shut my eyes and dreamt of the food that was being prepared'.

Erwan Helouri invited the merchant to step forward. Not wishing to escalate what he felt to be a dispute arising out of an accident of birth or circumstance and in order to avoid passing judgement against the vagabond which might have other adverse effects, he offered to make personal payment for the smells that had been so much enjoyed. Shaking some coins in his hands, which he held out in the direction of the merchant, Erwan commanded, *'Écoute'* (Listen).

Then again, he repeated the instruction and gesture, and again and again, *'Écoute ... écoute, écoute ding, dong'*.

Thoroughly puzzled and perplexed, the merchant waited in vain for the coins to be handed over to him as his compensation for the misdeeds of the vagabond. But to no avail. In words now familiar to French children who have heard the same tale, Erwan then explained, 'He has smelled your roasting meats; and you have heard the ring of my coins— let the sound pay for the smell!' Popular works depict a scene in which every one in the courtroom has a broad smile—with the exception that is of the downcast merchant.[4]

---

[4] Perhaps once this book is published, *'Écoute ... ding, dong'* might become a synonym/byword for base cause or worthless claim.

The rich man's bag of gold being thrust at the visitor as a form of temptation on the idyllic offshore island of Belle Isle (*Chapter 6*).

CHAPTER 4

Mediator, Counsellor, Lawyer, Judge

Erwan Helouri seated between a rich man and a poor man. This carving hangs in Quimper Cathedral, some 100 kilometres west of Tréguier. The Rennes diocese of which Erwan Helouri was at one time the judge extended over Quimper. It is nowadays the 'pottery capital' of Brittany, famous for its distinctive vases and tableware. Note that the litigants and judge in this picture are each holding a scroll or petition. Closer examination shows that the rich man—who shows great apprehension despite his outward sophistication—is holding a gold coin. I recall that whilst this photograph was being taken of what is a small item high on the wall in one of the less obvious parts of the cathedral, a crowd of onlookers began to form. By the time I left the building it was a key focus of attention, if not quite hysteria or frenzy, as it was enthusiastically captured on cameras and video recorders!

CHAPTER 4

Mediator, Counsellor, Lawyer, Judge

Erwan Helouri's ability when dealing with disputes and his reputation for ensuring equality and balance is as much a product of his skill as a counsellor and mediator as it is of his training as a lawyer and judge. Like a growing number of modern-day practitioners, especially those who work within what are called adversarial systems of justice, there are times when he noticeably seeks to 'do justice better'.[1] His counselling is evident in his late-night sessions as a student when putting the world to rights with his friend and confidant Jehan (*Chapter 2*) as much as it was in later life. Essentially, in all that he does, Erwan seeks outcomes that avoid conflict and which carry an inherent sense of justice. There are no winners or losers—victims or offenders—simply people whose competing interests stand to be resolved and who, through sensitive treatment, understand and accept the fairness of various outcomes.

ST YVES THE LAWYER AND ADVOCATE

There are countless stories of St Yves's abilities as an advocate or spokesperson—and, by the same token, he became what the witnesses to the Papal Enquiry into his potential sainthood described as a 'brilliant and compelling preacher'.[2] As an advocate he became a representative, champion or campaigner in the wider sense in which it is understood today. No great legal insights are to be found in his activities as a lawyer, other than his perception that law is generally far too complicated perhaps

---

[1] *Doing Justice Better* (2007), Waterside Press, is the title of a book by David J Cornwell in which he argues that the adversarial system and punitive mind-set detract from doing justice. Many other books on restorative justice exist, examples of which appear at www.watersidepress.co.uk

[2] I have encountered a number of lawyers with this dual faculty, and/or who might also be fine actors.

and, indeed, he seems to have broken certain cardinal rules—albeit quite justifiably some people might think.

Ignoring the 'cab-rank' principle designed to ensure that anyone and everyone, no matter how 'deserving' or 'undeserving' can obtain representation if they are 'next in the queue' (or 'rank'), he chose to take on 'only the most wretched cases', always on the side of the poor and oppressed, seeking to defeat power and influence. In a move that might send shivers down the spine of modern-day cost-driven lawyers, it is said that in general he only took on the cases of those *who could not afford to pay*. He gave as one reason for doing so that this would not simply help the poor but it would not deprive his colleagues of their living—which, it seems, would have caused him equal concern. There are several references to St Yves having invented what we would nowadays call legal aid (see under *The Invention of Pro Bono Work* later in this chapter).

'Brilliant and miraculous advocacy'

The Papal Enquiry heard that Erwan's advocacy was not only 'brilliant', but 'miraculous'. So much so that a number of witnesses claimed that he had represented them in the far flung courts of Brittany simultaneously, on the same dates! As a result of these claims, the assessors took to keeping maps and calendars at the ready, to plot all his activities. It is part of his sainthood and the legend that he would materialise when and where he was needed most, what in modern popular culture might be described as a Perry Mason-style approach to his work.[3]

An instance often quoted in support of such claims is that where he turned up in the court at Tours to defend a woman who was about to be dispossessed of her home and belongings by a wealthy man who had entrusted a casket of gold to her for safe-keeping. A week later, the man's colleague, who had accompanied him when the original deposit was made, arrived to collect the casket, ostensibly with full authority to do so. The first man/owner then arrived to demand the gold; accusing his colleague of a fraud when he found that it was gone. Erwan, by skilful cross-examination, was able to establish that the two were rogues, working in tandem. They went to prison, while the woman kept her effects.

---

[3] Perry Mason was the central character in a long-running 1950s TV series of that name. His assistant would invariably burst into the courtroom at the critical moment with the key evidence that was vital to save the defence case.

The lawyers' saint—truth or hijack?

Arguably, lawyers do not deserve any monopoly with regard to Erwan Helouri—although it is understandable that they might wish to claim him as their exclusive property (supported by faultless arguments and reasons, quite naturally!). No greater evidence is needed of the power of lawyers as a body to espouse their own cause than to witness one of the 'challenges' that take place at my own Inn of Court, Gray's Inn in London, whereby would-be barristers attempt to argue that black is white and vice-versa. In reality, St Yves would seem to be a saint for all seasons.[4] But the skills for which Erwan Helouri is so often feted have much more in common with the resolution of conflict and avoidance of unnecessary disputes than they have with legal or judicial reasoning itself.

JUDGE AT RENNES AND ELSEWHERE

The diocesan court at Rennes of which Erwan Helouri was placed in charge dealt with a mixture of criminal and civil matters. *Tous les process: vols, chicanes, expropriations, parjure, coups, calomnies …tous les sauf crimes*, words reasonably close to the English, but some, perhaps, needing translation: *vols*: thefts; *coups*: assaults, particularly with a weapon; *calomnies*: a generic term for libels and slanders. Immediately Erwan established a reputation for wise decision-making, concise judgements and listening to the briefest and best-honed pleas put forward by the advocates appearing before him in response to his reputation for giving them a fair and effective hearing.

Triumphant homecoming

By a convenient stroke of fortune, in 1283 Erwan Helouri was transferred from Rennes to become the judge—or magistrate[5]—in his home town of

---

[4] Despite St Yves' hard work, the general reputation of lawyers lingers on. A medieval joke relates how he arrives at the Gates of Heaven at the same time as a group of nuns. Heaven is overrun with nuns and they are told to wait. Turning to St Yves, St Peter enquires of his own background, to which St Yves replies, 'I am a lawyer, sir'. 'Then enter straightaway,' says St Peter, 'you are the first of those we have ever had'.

[5] These terms are used indiscriminately in the source materials. Nothing appears to turn on this and it would be wrong to compare ancient and modern-day terminology, especially in different countries.

Tréguier. Pictures and paintings depict him as an heroic figure, entering the town astride a white horse, to be greeted by crowds in the streets with cries which in translation come out as, 'Little Erwan!'; 'He hasn't changed a bit, I still recognise him'; and even, 'Just like his mother!'

Historic confessional booths in Tréguier Cathedral—indicative of a propensity for sin maybe: *Chapter 3*. There are other fine examples of the work of master craftsmen throughout the building.

He continued as a judge, in much the same informal style as before, until 1287 when he resigned his legal position to become a parish priest, first at Tredez and later at Louvannec. He was to continue in this role—albeit with frequent contact and associations with Tréguier and in regular demand as a mediator. In 1303, having foretold his own death to a gypsy—an unusual reversal of roles—he was carried to the cathedral, where, on May 19, he died, smiling so it is said, from natural causes.

THE INVENTION OF *PRO BONO* WORK

As a judge, St Yves is represented in pictures, carvings and statues—and nowadays in porcelain, pendants and all the other accoutrements of the gift shop—holding a scroll of legal documents, whilst rejecting a purse. As described in earlier chapters, this is the receiving of the poor man's petition, the rejection of the rich man's purse, or more generally any form or perquisite. He has no official symbol in art, as some saints do.

None of the rich men who sought to bribe the court ever seem to have been proceeded against for their dubious attempts to pervert the course of justice—thereby avoiding the need for such symbolic reminders of what, in justice terms, should be self-evident. Neither does anyone appear to have commented that a bias in favour of the poor, as opposed to equality of treatment, is, on principle, as objectionable as any other kind of bias. Either St Yves was unusual in adjudicating 'without fear', if with 'a degree of favour', albeit of an excusable kind, in which case he was only doing right whilst his brethren were not; or he was only doing what a judge should do anyway. No doubt, this is to entirely misunderstand the culture of the times. It was only in the 1880s that Britain finally made its own transition from what was dubbed 'basket justice', in which contributions might be placed in a basket positioned in front of the court bench.

But it was with those people who did not pay bribes—and, indeed, those people who could not afford to pay bribes—that St Yves is most associated. Whether acting as a judge, lawyer, mediator or counsellor he would do so without charge (or might in some cases ensure that the costs were picked up by someone who could afford to pay). It is claimed by some people that this is the origin of what is known as *pro bono* work, work that is done by lawyers (or other professional people) without charge. It is something that still occurs regularly in many jurisdictions including in the

UK and USA (where many death penalty cases are so conducted). Still others have interpreted St Yves' largesse as being a trigger for the spread of systems of legal aid, even though the difference here is that the lawyer's fee and account are charged to and paid for by the state (or maybe in some instances a charity) rather than the client himself or herself.

Another recurring motif: a woman holding up her child for a blessing—here in the form of a statue in the civic offices at Tréguier. The image is repeated countless times across Brittany and beyond. The original legend tells of children brought to Erwan Helouri for blessing and of cures or the acquisition by children so blessed of new qualities, abilities, powers and such.

CHAPTER 5

Miracle Worker

The ornate 'marbled-over' tomb of St Yves with the sun striking down through tall Gothic windows. The original tomb was destroyed in the aftermath of the French Revolution. For hundreds of years it has been a place of pilgrimage as evidenced by the tributes described in *Chapter 6*.

CHAPTER 5

Miracle Worker

Even taking into account the immaculate antecedents and achievements of Erwan Helouri described so far in this book, it remains debatable whether the campaign for his sainthood would have met the standards required for a positive assessment by the Papal Enquiry. But that enquiry was to hear about further miracles which, so it was claimed, he was responsible for or that occurred in his presence. Earlier chapters have touched upon Erwan's seeming ability to ensure the necessities of life, whether for himself, his associates or other people (as for example in *Chapter 2* when he sat down with his Breton bagpipes to charm money for food from passers-by), and his ability to materialise as an advocate and represent different clients in two or more places at the same time (*Chapter 4*). Some accounts of the witnesses to the enquiry reported that the same applied to his later work as a priest, in that he frequently preached or ministered to people in diverse places at the self-same time. Taken together and in combination, such items may have carried some weight, but further and more tangible evidence—if that is not a contradiction in terms—was required. And as any lawyer who has dealt with cross-examination and close scrutiny of the recollections of witnesses knows, the memory can be quite fallible. Events of whatever kind—whether styled 'miracle' or not—often have competing explanations.

WEIGHING THE EVIDENCE

Additional evidence told of times when supplies for the hospital that Erwan Helouri founded in Tréguier were completely exhausted, but the medicine chests became full and kitchen cupboards brimming with fresh produce after he had paid a visit. Other evidence concerned a young crippled boy who was immediately cured and able to dispense with his crutches after he had touched Erwan's body as it lay in the cathedral. The cure, so it was claimed, took place before and was observed by the assembled throng. One remarkable account told of a vision, said to be of

Jesus Christ himself, who, on one festive occasion, appeared in the guise of a beggar to ask for food at the high table in the Bishop's Palace.

The Christian Aid web-site[1] in its 'A-Z of Saints' describes St Yves somewhat peremptorily as follows, but manages a reference to one miracle:

> This Breton nobleman became a lawyer noted for defending the poor free of charge [and was] also known for his asceticism. In later life he became a preacher and founded a hospital. He was also said to have performed a miracle by feeding hundreds with a loaf of bread.

This and many comparable incidents were listened to and studied by the assessors. The claims were legion. As with that involving the loaf of bread already mentioned above, they attract biblical comparisons. According to *The Golden Legend*,[2] these ranged from the raising of 14 people from the dead in various places, including 'two children living within their mother's womb and dead before their baptisim which ... received life', to the delivery of ten mad folk from wicked spirits. Similarly:

> Thirteen people who had contracted or were filled with paralysis were ... restored to good health. Three blind people were made able to see. Various folk, in ten places, all with their goods, were kept and saved from drowning in the sea. One person ... filled with dropsy was entirely cured. Another that had [a gall]stone [as] great as an egg ... was brought back to health. One person condemned to be hanged fell three times from the gallows, and [still alive and well] was delivered and let go.[3] A woman [devoid of milk] within her breasts [found that they became] filled with it. Things lost by various people in diverse

---

[1] www.surefish.co.uk/faith/features/saints

[2] *The Golden Legend* is a unique medieval hagiography on the lives of the saints, Jacobus de Voragine, c.1260. 'Legenda' or 'what is read' is from the Latin *legere*, to read. From 1470 to 1530, *The Golden Legend* was reputedly the most printed book in Europe. First translated in the Caxton English version of 1483 (updated in 1900 by F S Ellis), it is quaint and archaic. St Yves figures in Volume 7, seemingly a variant of the evidence to the Papal Enquiry. The quotations in the text above have been reworded by the author of this work, keeping to the sense of the original, longer extracts from which appear in an appendix. Other useful sources are *Butler's Lives of the Saints* (various editions and publishers over two centuries) and *The Saints of Brittany* (Undated), Spence L, Kessinger Publishing, USA.

[3] There are various accounts of failed executions from around the world, many attracting theories of divine intervention or divine justice, such as the famous English case of John Lee at Exeter Prison in 1885.

places were found and recovered by miracles. Two dumb children and various others that had lost the use of the tongue were given back their speech.

Healing the sick

Other examples included women who were giving birth being 'delivered from the peril of death'; fires being put out and people saved; and corn multiplying in its store, including in the garret of Erwan Helouri, but also of other people. In similar vein, 'many sick folk were healed after touching his hood. A man dressing the wheel of his water-mill, on whom suddenly the water came from high rushing … was saved from drowning …'.

A miraculous construction and a transformation

Once when workmen were building a bridge they discovered that a post they were about to use was some half a metre short. They prayed to the saint and the post was then found to be of the exact length that was required. On other occasions, when Erwan had given away all of his bread to poor people, loaves appeared and were brought to him by them, enough for his own needs, and once 'by a woman unknown [who then] vanished … and never was seen [again]'. Yet another time, Erwan:

> received a poor man appearing right foul and disfigured, in filthy clothing, and had him eat [from Erwan's] own dish … this poor man departing and saying: 'God be with you' and … his gown that before was wonderfully foul … became so white, and so greatly resplendent and shining, and his face so fair appeared and so bright, that all the house was replenished and filled with great light.

The death of the Archbishop of Narbonne

According to the same chain of evidence Erwan was responsible for restoring the Archbishop of Narbonne who had suffered from 'a strong ague' ('was vexed with a strong axe' in the original). The Archbishop was:

> … by the feebleness of his nature … reputed and holden as for dead … for his eyes were shut in [the] manner of a dead man. At the invocation or calling to Saint Ives … by his parents and friends, with weepings, vows, devotions, was the [a]foresaid archbishop through the merits of the saint restored unto life, sight and good health ….

Every such consideration was documented in fine detail by the assessors to be reported back to Rome together with notes of his other, personal; attributes and accomplishments. As a result, in 1347, plain Erwan Helouri was canonised by Pope Clement VI and became St Yves Helouri of Kermartin, 'Friend of the Poor'. As is noted in *Chapter 6* his patronage extended not just to lawyers and judges but to a range of other groups. By the standards of sainthood this process of canonisation occurred only a relatively short time after his death.

MORE QUESTIONS THAN ANSWERS

The miracles were not just central to the decision to make Erwan Helouri a saint but also to his legend in general. In all the stories about him they go hand-in-hand with his standing as someone of unusual wisdom, fairness, perception and preparedness to stand up for the poor and disinherited. Yet there is a sense, as a lawyer or other detached investigator might say, in which they 'cloud the issue'. Clearly there will be those people for whom the existence of miracles is the decisive factor, and for whom Erwan's personal qualities and abilities are peripheral or marginal. After all, if miracles really did occur, what else is there to say? Yet without them, is everything lost—surely not?

It is quite possible to argue the case for immortalising Erwan Helouri or treating him as a paragon of fair and considerate treatment of others without any reference to the miracles whatsoever. Any lawyer arguing that less tangible events should be left to one side would no doubt seek to emphasise that evidence of miracles could be misleading, prejudicial or maybe perhaps unnecessary. This need not be seen as a heretical view: many readers of this book may simply be sceptical, non-believers or people for whom, whatever the talk of miracles, the standard of proof in relation to them will never be satisfied. Maybe there is a risk that events were affected by euphoria, hysteria or other forms of communal madness. Yet such a lawyer might well laud the fundamental and deserving qualities of justice, fairness and impartiality that the legend of St Yves necessarily rests on and imparts. Other people might see equal merit in his ability as a preacher and minister rather than as an advocate but remain unconvinced about ethereal matters. For people who believe in miracles, this might perhaps be regarded as a bonus. St Yves should, however, also attract a high level of respect from those who do not.

Intangible evidence

The many tributes laid at St Yves' tomb attest to a deep belief by many people that miracles did occur during his own time and that they continue into the present day. The tributes take the form of small marble plaques of the kind described in *Chapter 6*. They are overwhelmingly powerful in effect whether viewed individually or *en masse* and in a way that no rational interpretation of events can deny.

A statuette of St Yves standing by a model sailing boat of the kind once seen in the harbour at Tréguier—and one small corner of the countless tributes.

A fine example of a Breton half-timbered house.

CHAPTER 6

Tributes by the Score

St Yves in close-up.

CHAPTER 6

Tributes by the Score

To enter Tréguier Cathedral is to enter a different world. The descriptions given in earlier chapters gloss over its construction in a range of styles over the centuries. The overall design is Gothic, but there is a distinctive Romanesque tower over the transept. The great spire at its western end is from what is known as the Decorated period. A masterpiece in its own right, the spire is built of stone that has been fretted into multi-patterned holes which reduce wind resistance. Within the building there is stone vaulting without parallel and stained glass, mostly in the form of biblical illustrations, in over 70 windows. There are Renaissance choir stalls and to the rear of the building a 15th century cloister populated by stone effigies, each lying down on a rough stone plinth (see the photograph on page xi).

IMAGES AND MESSAGES

A variety of images immediately force themselves on the eye. Not least amongst these are the dramatically positioned twin statues to the right and left of the nave and towering some five metres into the air: the one of St Yves, the other of St Tugdall who is mentioned towards the end of this chapter. Yet more prominent in its effect, positioned just to one side of the main aisle, is the tomb of St Yves.[1] This ornate construction is a replica of the original that was destroyed in the French Revolution, when much of Brittany was ransacked in the name of the Republic in its relentless and escalating search for royalist sympathisers. There is something quite perverse in the idea that St Yves was, in effect, categorised as being on the side of the aristocracy, an indicator perhaps of how badly wrong things must have been going by that time. He seems to have been more of a renegade and to have understood the ills of privilege and patronage far more acutely than many a French citizen or revolutionary.

---

[1] 'St Yves' tomb' also has another meaning as described later in the chapter.

Grateful lawyers, clients and other beneficiaries

Just beside the tomb, votes of thanks, lighted candles (known as 'votive candles') and plaques bear testimony to the deeds and miracles that St Yves is credited with, not simply in the past, but on a daily and ongoing basis. Many of these items have been placed at the foot of the tomb by generations of grateful lawyers along with flowers (or what are sometimes described as 'posies'). Some have messages attached: attesting to events that have turned out favourably for the person concerned, others recording outright gratitude. The acknowledgements are numerous and various in their origins, content and mode of expression. A general feature is their unquestionably heartfelt nature and lack of all doubt. Each and every message is from someone who is convinced that he or she has been helped by St Yves in some significant way after he or she appealed—or maybe prayed—to him for help. Mostly, the tributes take the form of small marble plaques with gold lettering, often bearing the name of St Yves and the single word '*Merci*'.

Many of the tributes are indeed from lawyers or their grateful clients, often with a clear reference to justice or the workings of the law or legal system. There are also messages from people who say that they or someone connected to them have been cured or 'saved'. With others it may not always be clear why thanks are being given, but the general import of all these tributes is that St Yves somehow materialised to assist or had a remote hand in the shaping of events. There are similar references to the poor, but not nearly so many as those from grateful lawyers or their clients.

THE PARDON OF ST YVES

Tréguier was once the capital of Trégor, the local 'region' or *département* within Britanny, a role now filled by Lannion to the west. Tréguier overlooks the head of the River Jaudy estuary where an inlet, sheltered by tall hills on both sides, allows for the safe anchorage of sardine boats, yachts, small cargo ships and other seafaring craft. Two tall stone towers act as a reminder of former fortifications. Tréguier's medieval status as a centre of the arts and education is still echoed in the galleries and craft shops as well as the elaborate design of many older buildings. The whole town comes alive each year to celebrate its favourite son.

A torchlit procession

Every year, on May 19, the date of Erwan Helouri's death at Minihy-Tréguier (in 1253) or the nearest Sunday to that date, an elaborate ceremony marks the Pardon of St Yves during which a torchlit procession is joined by upwards of 10,000 lawyers, judges and representatives of the legal and judicial professions of France and other countries, many of those attending dressed in their fine robes. The procession moves on foot from Tréguier to Mehiny Tréguier, his birthplace and final home,[2] a journey known as 'Going to St Yves'.[3] It is irresistable to comment that they are dressed in the very kind of attire that Erwan Helouri rejected, so that the money might be better spent on the poor (*Chapter 4*). But they do go on foot, which he would have welcomed wholeheartedly.

The relics of the saint

A small church stands at Minihy-Tréguier. Those making the pilgrimage to it are expected to scramble through its low, 13th century archway, also known as 'St Yves' tomb', this being his original resting place before his body was taken to the cathedral. The commemorative photographs always depict one or two British and American lawyers and judges within the long procession. On these occasions, the relics of the saint, a term which in St Yves's case includes his skull and the remnants of his bones, are taken from their place of safekeeping and carried, shoulder high, in a small, gilded display cabinet, or 'reliquary'.

Those in the procession unite in a single purpose. No one asks questions of the kind raised in the last chapter of this book. Everyone is immersed in the legend and paying obedient homage to the saint. They do not look poor. The feasting goes on all night. What St Yves would have made of it is difficult to say. The 16,000 or so inhabitants of Tréguier, swelled to almost double that number by visitors attending the celebratory weekend, are rightly proud of St Yves, even if he may not yet have achieved the global or household-word status that some of the more enthusiastic promotional literature might imply.

---

[2] Minihy-Tréguier is a delightful village, but its surrounds have been largely overtaken by vehicle showrooms and car lots, part of a still expanding out-of-town retail complex.

[3] See my comments in the *Epilogue* about the use of this phrase, which is reminiscent of that used in an (unconnected) English riddle.

The spire of Tréguier Cathedral with its fretwork to enhance wind resistance.

VARIATIONS ON A THEME

Some indication of a more complicated version of events has already been hinted at in the account of the miracles of St Yves given in *Chapter 5*. Indeed, some accounts and tributes contain embellished versions of almost every aspect of the legend. Thus, e.g. there are tales about the extent to which Erwan Helouri pursued a rigorously simple and devoted life, of his wearing hair-shirts or other coarse clothing, of his ministering to people in prison or facing trial, his choice of the most deformed people and vagabonds as companions, and of his extended fasting. Certain accounts speak of him being wholly resistant to the blasphemies that were regularly hurled at him by some passers-by, yet 'when men did mock him or said evil to him, he answered nothing, but ... sustained their evil words patiently and with great joy'.

Fasting and abstaining
Certain accounts claim that in later life he abstained from meat and fasted on bread and water on Mondays, Wednesdays and Fridays, often throughout Advent and Lent, and at other times for up to seven days at a time—and that when he did eat he would consume the most basic of foods, rough brown bread and a pottage made from leftovers, herbs, beans and incorporating such ingredients as radish roots.[4] He rejected alcohol except when conducting mass and communion, but in his own true fashion would, if pressed to dine with bishops and the like, colour his water with a splash from the carafe so as not to offend his host.

A variety of roles
There are also variations concerning the causes of which St Yves is patron. Whilst, as described in *Chapter 1*, he is generally and most often described as the patron saint of lawyers, there are other references to his occupying that same role in relation to advocates, abandoned people, bailiffs, barristers (as opposed to every type of lawyer), Brittany itself, canon law, the law in general, judges, justice, jurists, notaries, orphans and the poor, wretched and miserable. Some accounts say that he joined

---

[4] Certain modern-day experts claim a basic and frugal 'monk's diet' is amongst the most healthy and that an abstemious life is largely for the better!

or was closely associated with a Franciscan order[5] at Guingamp and further stress his frugal approach to living, endless charity and how he would 'eschew all vanities'. Others emphasise his unbridled energy and capacity to go without sleep for long periods of time, his campaigns against taxation by the King or in support of the rights of the Church, his later work as a priest in the parishes of Tredez and Louvannec, or his abilities as an arbitrator and mediator. I would like to think that had the term been around he would have been closely associated with forms of what is nowadays termed restorative justice (with which, in his various roles, he seems to have been naturally in tune, especially when seeking to resolve competing interests whilst avoiding discord and strife).

Symbols, emblems and *bon mots*
There are similar variations in relation to the symbolism with which St Yves is associated. This generally focuses on legal scrolls or books and the juxtaposition of the trappings of wealth and poverty. Whilst the common imagery is of him between a rich man and a poor man as described in earlier chapters, he is also sometimes depicted in a *mortier* (the cap worn by French lawyers on formal occasions) and robes surrounded by doves of peace with an angel at his head and a lion (for strength) or dog (for faithfulness) at his feet, or sometimes a cat (for watchfulness) and a loaf of bread (concern for the poor). There are accounts of him giving away his clothes as he walked the streets (and corresponding tales of those same clothes being mysteriously replaced as he continued on his way). Yet other accounts identify him as 'The Honest Lawyer' (*sic*) (or *St Yves de Vérité*) as if this were a feat so unique in itself as to call for canonization in its own right!

In Erwan Helouri's own time the legal system is said to have been so endemically corrupt that it actually operated through a system of bribes and inducements (and some people would point out that all such systems, even in the modern-day, are always open to departures from ethical standards unless there are careful checks and balances). Hence, one commonly quoted reference to him, said to date from the 14th century, seeks to emphasise that whilst he might be the patron saint of lawyers he may not, in truth, be their definitive model or blueprint:

---

[5] Which would tally with his studies under Thomas Aquinas as described in *Chapter 2*.

Sanctus Ivo erat Brito,
Advocatus et non latro,
Res Miranda populo.

These sentiments occur in several different original forms and varying translations but can be roughly taken to mean:

St Yvo [Yves] was a lawyer/Breton/ate no/lived in the land of beef,
But was not dishonest/no thief,
An astonishing thing to behold/in people's eyes/to believe.

None of these variations, perspectives or embellishments detracts from the more straightforward accounts given in earlier chapters and in modern times they can perhaps be viewed as part and parcel of the minor industry that has developed around the legend. But they can sometimes provide a fresh line of enquiry for anyone who is interested in pursuing matters in greater detail.

A DIFFERENT CAUSE FOR CELEBRATION

The town of Tréguier does have a place in world fame and another cause for celebration, but this time as the birthplace of a more wayward son and one who is seemingly less talked about locally. It is the home of Ernest Renan (1823-92), the much acclaimed French philosopher, thinker, historian, academic and rationalist.

Ernest Renan
Renan, whilst he repudiated a charge of atheism, was responsible for several works directly challenging orthodox Christian beliefs. When, in 1903, the French government erected a statue to his memory at Tréguier, it was against fierce opposition from the townspeople, largely orthodox Roman Catholics and strong supporters of St Yves. The cathedral and statue now stand side-by-side in eternal conflict, the effigy of Renan only, as the crow flies, some 50 metres from the tomb of the saint across Place du Martray, a broad square surrounded by attractive old Breton buildings, cafés and shops. According to one tourist brochure: 'If you have a taste for small local museums, Ernest Renan's house is worth a visit and provides some fascinating insights into the traditional culture of small-town Brittany'!

Renan, a Jew, was the author of *La Vie de Jésus* ('The Life of Jesus'), published in 1863, which controversially denied the supernatural element in the life of Jesus Christ. It was the first work in a series on the history of the origins of Christianity. The ever present and critical Renan still looks down on St Yves' resting place from across the square. Perhaps on a cold night the two ghosts come face-to-face, Erwan Helouri inviting the shivering Renan into his Gothic home—to share a poor man's meal, perhaps, and to pursue a sleepless night exchanging points of view.

THE WELSH MONK

Finally, I have mentioned in the *Introduction* that the monastery at Tréguier out of which the town and cathedral developed was founded by a Welshman. His name was St Tugdual (variously Tudwall or sometimes Tugdall) a 9th century monk who left Wales for Brittany to spread the Gospel. As mentioned earlier, within the cathedral itself the statues of both saints, St Yves and St Tugdall, stand side-by-side some ten metres apart to either side of the nave where each is seemingly lost in his own separate and detached world.

Tréguier is generally regarded as having been founded by St Tugdall. It became an independent diocese 300 years later and by St Yves' time (in the late 13th and early 14th century) it was already a place of some significance and refinement. That which was begun by St Tugdall was further enhanced by Erwan Helouri's widespread fame and grand plans for the cathedral after he took up residence there.

Epilogue

St Yves between a rich man and a poor man in the porch at Tréguier.

Epilogue

I am, by my own admission, an unlikely pilgrim. But for an accidental detour some years ago now, I might never have heard of Erwan Helouri. Fortunately, at the time, my children were of an age when anything that sounded faintly morbid had a head start over counter-attractions—and once there was a mention of St Yves's bones being paraded through the streets even they began to take an interest. For quite different reasons, I found myself drawn back to the place and I remain captivated and intrigued by the legend of St Yves.

A deceptively simple story
As can be seen from the earlier chapters of this book, the legend is a simple tale, almost like a fairy story at times. But it has many layers. I suppose that my main interest is with the one which deals with St Yves as a lawyer, judge, arbitrator and mediator along with issues of fairness and justice. It is fascinating that the importance and significance of such matters was recognised such a long time ago, if not sooner, since Erwan Helouri took his ideas from certain earlier sources as mentioned in *Chapter 2* and his wisdom naturally invites comparison with that of King Solomon of *Old Testament* fame. It is intriguing that values of the kind noted in this book have existed across time, language, cultures and national boundaries. Despite the obvious religious connotations of the story, these values are also recognisable in a modern-day and increasingly secular society. They do not depend on mystique or the supernatural, even if the legend of St Yves itself relies on miracles to reinforce it.

Decency, integrity and ethics
Erwan Helouri can be viewed as a renegade lawyer, official and mediator albeit one who operated within the system rather than by attacking it wholesale from without. But I prefer to see in him something else, which I think is what triggered my interest in the first place. He is in the tradition of the great social and penal reformers, especially those who took a personal stand or who sought to convince people by example. It is not hard to think of people (or organizations) who have been vilified for this in modern times (as St Yves himself was by some people, as described in *Chapter 6*). Anyone who argues, for example, in support of human rights or better treatment for

prisoners or improved ways of doing justice (such as restorative justice that relies on repairing harm as between victims and offenders rather than punishment *per se*) risks a similar fate. Yet the importance of such matters and of values such as decency, integrity and ethics is paramount. Whatever detractors and people with slick solutions may say, societies soon disintegrate once politicians, officials or practitioners lose sight of basic values—as to which there is no want of historical and modern examples from various places around the world.

Facing East: a stained glass window depicts the two local saints.

Justice depends on narrowing inequalities
This, I think, is why I would like to see the story of Erwan Helouri writ large, as a reminder that it may sometimes be necessary to go against the grain—as I have heard some people describe the phenomenon—in order to maintain values that (whatever some elements of the media might have us believe) are intrinsically sound and which have stood the test of time. The legend of St Yves can be seen as a reference point or beacon, a reminder of this. It also emphasises that social justice involves a narrowing of inequalities and serves to encourage those people who, like Erwan Helouri, reject false distinctions, arguments or outcomes.

It is sometimes necessary to scratch beneath the surface. The fine clothes or words of judges, lawyers, politicians, officials, arbitrators and the like should never be allowed to obscure the true nature of events. To sit in one of the cafés on the edge of the Place du Martray in the centre of Tréguier, to soak up the legend and to observe the pageant of events described in *Chapter 3*—in which two noticeably different worlds seem to collide—is to experience this at first hand.

St Tudual, or Tudwall, or Tugdall: page 70.

BACK IN THE UK

There is another well-known Yves (or Ivo) who hails from Brittany and with whom St Yves de Tréguier should not be confused. Yves de Chartres was a *lawyer* but *not* a saint. He lived in the eleventh century, wrote about canon law and was a bishop and theologian. More naturally perhaps, most English people to whom I have mentioned St Yves think immediately of the seaside resort of St Ives in Cornwall or possibly of the small market town of St Ives in what was formerly Huntingdonshire but is now Cambridgeshire.

Separated only by the broader reaches of the English Channel, Cornwall is not unlike parts of Brittany and there are many parallels other than geography. Its association with legend, ghosts, romance, tradition and separatism is not unlike that of its French counterpart, and it is perhaps not surprising that, unless explanation is offered, many people on hearing of St Yves de Tréguier assume that there is some connection between St Ives in Cornwall and the subject matter of this book. But this is not so, any more than there is a connection with St Ives in Cambridgeshire or the children's riddle:

> As I was going to St. Ives I met a man with seven wives,
> Each wife had seven sacks, each sack had seven cats,
> Each cat had seven kits: kits, cats, sacks and wives,
> How many were going to St. Ives?[1]

St Ives, Cornwall
The 5th or maybe 6th century St Ia (or Hya) — as she was originally called — is said to have been a woman of noble birth who drifted across the Irish Sea and into Cornish waters on a leaf that had been miraculously enlarged to serve as a coracle (a primitive form of boat). She was one of 24 children of the Irish King Brychan, all of whom were driven by missionary zeal and founded churches across 'Celtic Lands'. She is often put forward as a Cornish version of St Valentine, the patron saint of sweethearts.

According to the great Victorian novelist Thomas Hardy when he described his first experience of Cornwall in 1870, 'The place is pre-eminently the region of dream and mystery'. Even today something of a mystical quality not unlike that in Brittany continues to exert a strange influence over those who visit its often hidden and solitary places, as did the Poet Laureate, Sir John Betjeman who is buried at St. Enodoc Church, Trebetherick, close to St Ives and who noted that 'A million years or

---

[1] To which the answer is not 2,801 but 'at least one, the person asking the question plus anyone who happens to be travelling in the same direction as him or her'. The rhyme first appeared in print around 1730 and appears to refer to St Ives in Cornwall. The use of the term 'Going to St. Yves', which most people in Britain would immediately connect with the rhyme is mentioned in a Breton context on page 65 — where it signifies attending the Pardon of St Yves.

unrelenting tide/Have smoothed the strata of the great cliffside'.[2] Cornish myths and legends include those of Jack the Giant Killer, The Lost Land of Lyonesse and The Lady of the Lake all of which evoke a backdrop and symbolism akin to that of North-west France.[3]

The author scrutinises another source.

St Ives, Cambridgeshire

The township of St Ives was originally the village of Slepe (meaning 'muddy' in Anglo-Saxon). In 1001 AD, so the story goes, the corpse of St Ivo was discovered in a stone coffin or sarcophagus (possibly Roman in origin) in those parts. St Ivo was a Persian bishop who visited Britain with a view to converting the natives to Christianity. His bones were

---

[2] 'By the Ninth Green at St Enodoc', *High and Low* (1966).
[3] For further details, see, e.g. www.connexions.co.uk/culture.

taken to nearby Ramsey Abbey where they were placed in a shrine, whilst a small monastery was built on the exact spot where they were found, which became the re-named St Yvo's Priory.

It is thought that this St Ives (the spelling changing with the passing of time) dates from the 6th or 7th century. The body was identified by a silver chalice and remnants of the insignia of someone of Episcopal rank — and also, so the legend continues, due the vision of a local man who described someone wearing the robes and ornaments of a bishop. When asked who he was, the man identified himself as St Ivo and asked to be transported to the abbey.

STOP PRESS

Things sometimes have a strange way of unravelling. As this book was going to press an advertising flyer landed on my desk concerning a new edition of a work that last appeared over two hundred years ago and that is about to be published in France. It is the first part of a new history series based on medieval sources and manuscripts and is called *Yvo Haelori*, which is yet another variation on Erwan Helouri or St Yves to those described in *Chapters 1* and *5*. The book is in French and contains what are described as *Monuments originaux de l'histoire de saint Yves*, or a collection of ancient documents and papers and other information appertaining to him.[4]

The book that you are reading is and remains the only one in the English language, or so I believe. I would also like to think it is the first book, whenever written or in whatever language, that seeks to convey why it is that the story of St Yves resonates — or should resonate — across cultures and in both ancient and modern times. There are often no real winners in legal or other conflicts and anyone who can retain the goodwill of both parties or induce a sense of fairness and justice in those who by the very nature of decision-making must lose out deserves recognition on that count alone. The more cases that can be settled out-of-court the better. I very much hope that Erwan Helouri will find many new friends.

---

[4] *Yvo Haelori* (2008), Deuffic, J L, Pecia, France.

Appendix I

Extracts from *The Golden Legend*

Appendix *The Golden Legend*

As intimated in *Chapter 5*, *The Golden Legend* is an early—and by current standards somewhat quaint and primitive—record of the lives of the saints. It was first published in 1260 and first translated into English in the Caxton version of 1483 and modernised in 1990 by F S Ellis although many words and forms still serve to defeat all but the closest of study. An entry concerning St Yves appears in Volume 7, from which the following extracts are taken.

At times, the translation does not always carry, at least in terms of modern-day English and a number of footnotes have thus been inserted in relation to extreme examples. This said, the story outlined in this book is easily discernible, whilst reading it in the original can sometimes trigger new insights and add context.

The original was printed as a virtually continuous whole. In what follows, the text has been broken up into convenient paragraphs for ease of reading and comprehension.

S. Ives[1] was born in little Britain in the diocese of Trygvier, engendered or begotten of parents noble and catholic, and it was revealed to his mother in her sleep that he should be sanctified. In his first age he was of right good conditions, and right humbly and devoutly frequented the churches, hearing ententively the masses and the sermons. Much of his time he employed to study busily the holy letters, and read much curiously the lives of the saints, and pained himself much with all his power for to ensue them, the which by process of time was adorned of right great wisdom and renowned full of great science both in right civil and in canon law, and also in theology well lettered as it appeared sith, as well in contemplation and judgment, as giving counsel to the souls upon the fait of their conscience.

For after that he had occupied and exercised much holily and devoutly the fait of advocacy in the bishop's court of Trygvier, ever pleading

---

[1] The spelling that is used throughout this ancient document.

without taking any salary the causes of the miserable and poor persons, exposing himself to it with his good gree,[2] and not required by them for to defend their questions and differences, he was chosen into the office of the official, first in the court of the archdeacon of Rennes, and afterwards in the said court of the bishop of Trygvier, which lawfully, justly, and diligently accomplished all such things that be pertaining to the said office. He succoured them that were oppressed and that had had wrong, and to every each one rendered his own by right, without any acception[3] or taking of money, nor none other good. The which then, called to the government and guiding of souls, bare ever with him the Bible and his breviary or portos, and so he, made and ordained in the order of priesthood, celebrated as every day, and heard much humbly, devoutly, and dilgently the confessions of his parishioners.

He visited the sick folk without difference, and recomforted them right wisely, and taught to them the way of their salvation, and devoutly administered unto them ...

What marvel he was of admirable or wonderful humility which he showed over all in habit or clothing, in deed, in words, going, coming, and being in divers companies. He spake ever to the folk both more and less sweetly, and full meekly looking on the earth, his hood before his face, that he should not be praised of the folk and to eschew all vanities. And by the space of fifteen years before his death he ne ware[4] but coarse cloth, russet or white, such as poor folk of the country be accustomed to wear.

He held the ewer and also the towel while the poor washed their hands, and after with his own hands administered to them the meat that they should eat, and setting himself on the ground ate with them of the said meat, that is to wit brown bread, and sometimes a little pottage. And among them that ate with him he had no prerogative, but the most deformed and most miserable he set nigh him.

---

[2] Seemingly a variant of 'agreeably', or a word signifying zest or enthusiasm.
[3] Without accepting any payment.
[4] Never wore other than coarse cloth, etc.

He lay all night on the ground and had for his bedding, for sheets, for coverlet, and for hanging, only a little straw. Ever before the celebration of his mass, ere he revested him, he kneeled down before the altar, and devoutly made his prayer, weeping and piteously sighing, and oft-times as he celebrated his mass plenty of tears fell from his eyes along his face. The humility of whom pleased much unto our Lord as once it appeared by a columbe or dove of marvellous splendour which openly was seen flying within the church of Trygvier about the altar, where this holy S. Ives said mass.[5] And certainly full patiently he suffered all injuries and blasphemies, for when men did mock him or said evil to him, he answered nothing, but having his thought on God sustained their evil words patiently and with great joy.

A man he was of tranquillity, for he loved peace, and never he was moved to no strife, indignation, or ire for nothing that ever was done to him. He said no words tumelous or contumelious, ne other disordinate words.

He was defensor, without dread, of the liberties of the church, whereof it happed that as a sergeant of the king's had taken and led with him the bishop's horse of Trygvier for the encheson of the centime of the goods of the foresaid bishop, S. Ives then being in the office of official, virtuously took the said horse join the said sergeant and led him again unto the bishop's place. And how be it that men deemed and weened that great evil or damage should fall therefor, as well to S. Ives as to the church, seeing that the sergeant was about to have procured it, nevertheless no manner of damage came never thereof, neither to the saint nor to the church. Which thing was holden and reputed for a miracle, and not without cause attributed to the merits of the said S. Ives, for it is believed and testified that he was chaste both of flesh and in thought all the time of his life, and also chaste both in words and of eyes, and lived always so honestly and so chastely that never no tokens of worldly manners appeared on him, but certainly ever he abhorred and cursed the sin of lechery, and he being accustomed to preach against the said sin, made many a person to flee from it.

---

[5] Sometimes quoted as a miracle.

He was never found slothful ne negligent, but ever ready to orison or predication, or else he was studying in the holy scriptures or doing works of charity and pity ...

He treated to right the word of virtue and of truth, and ever eschewing all vain words, spake but little and with pain, save the words of God and of salvation perdurable. And he, preaching the word of God right well and boldly, brought oft them that heard him to compunction of heart and evermore unto tears, and he exercising and occupying him in this holy operation or work thereas he might be heard by the leave of the bishops and diocesans, ever going on foot, preached sometimes upon a day in four churches, much far from one another.[6] And to the end that he should not leave the custom of his abstinence, he after this great labour returned fasting unto his house, and would never accord with no man to dine with him.

He had the spirit of prophecy, for he prophesied that a recluse should be seen among men by the vice of covetise. The which thing happed not long after, for the meschant recluse leaving the way of salvation and of penitence, went out from his cell, and took a worldly and damnable way. This holy S. Ives laboured ever to appease all discordance and strife after his power, and the folk which might not accord by his persuasion and admonishings, were called soon to concord after his orison by him made to God.

It may not be recounted, ne never it was seen in our time, the great charity, pity, and misericorde that he had towards the poor indigent and suffretous, towards the widows and to the poor children both fatherless and motherless all the time of his life. All that he received or might have, as well of the church as of his patrimony, he gave to them before said without any difference, when he was dwelling at Rennes, and promoted to the office of official there at the court of the archdeacon. Also ere he changed his manner of living, he made upon the great and solemn holidays plenty of meat to be dressed and ready for to eat, and at dinner-time he called and made to be called the poor folk to dinner, and to them

---

[6] Reflecting his reputation as a lawyer, as a preacher the suggestion is that he might be in different places around the same time: *Chapter 5*.

administered meat with his own hands, and after, he ate with two poor children which for the love of our Lord Jesu Christ he sustained at school, for ever he was right courteous to help children, both father- and motherless, and as their father sent them to school, and with his own sustained them and paid also the salary to their masters.

He revested right courteously the poor naked of our Lord. It happed once that a gown and a hood both of like cloth which he had do make for himself to wear, and so he taking greater care of the poor naked than of his own body, gave the said gown and hood to a poor man. He held hospitality indifferently for the poor pilgrims in a house which he did make for the nonce,[7] to the which he administered both meat and drink, bed and fire for to warm them in winter. In wheresoever a place that he went the suffretous and poor, that ran to him from all sides, followed him, for all that he had was ready to their behoof as their own.

He gave sudaries for to bury with the dead bodies, and with his own hands helped to bury them. A poor man once came against him, and he having as then nothing ready to give him, took his hood and gave it to the said poor man, and went home barehead. He chastised his flesh much sharply, for he was so accustomed to be in orisons and in prayers and to study, that the most part of the time he passed without sleep both day and night …

He ware ever the hair under his shirt, whiles that yet he was in the office of the official in the city of Trygvier. He used brown bread and porridge such as commonly use poor labourers, and none other meat he ne had, and to his drink used cold water, and there lived with such meat and drink by the space of eleven years, till he came to his death. He fasted eleven Lents and all the Advents of our Lord, and from the Ascension unto Pentecost, all ember days, all vigils of our Lady, and of the apostles, and all other days stablished by holy church for to fast, he fasted with bread and water. And above all this during the eleven years aforesaid, he fasted three days in the week with bread and water, that is to wit Wednesday, Friday, and Saturday, and on the other days he ate also but

---

[7] Presumably in the sense of 'an outsider of sorts' rather than in its modern-day sense of 'sex offender'.

once a day, and used bread and pottage, such as followeth except, the Sundays, Christmasday, Easterday, Whitsunday, and All Hallows' day, on which days he ate twice. His bread was rustical brown, made of barley or oats, his pottage was of great coles or of other herbs or beans, or of radish root savoured only with salt without any other liquor, sauf that sometimes he put in it a little flour and a little butter, and on Easterday above his accustomed pittance he ate two eggs.

He never within the space of fourteen years before his death tasted of no wine, save only at mass after that he had taken the body and blood of our Lord, or else sometime when he dined with the bishop, for then within his water he put a little wine only for to change the colour. He fasted once by the space of seven days without any meat or drink, ever being in good health.

The foresaid S. Ives lived fifty years or thereabout, and in his last sickness he ceased not to teach them that were about him, and he preached unto them of their salvation, and coming beneurely unto his last days, took humbly the sacraments of the body of our Lord and last unction, lying on his noble bed beforesaid, adjusted always to the same with great instance of his friends, a little straw. Three days before his death he had on his hood instead of kerchief about his head, and had on his gown, and refusing all other things, he was covered with a little and bad coverlet, saying that he was not worthy to have any other parements on him. The pure and clean saint then, having the hair on his flesh, covered with his shirt and issuing out of this world in the year of grace thirteen hundred and three, the nineteenth day of May, that was on the Sunday after the Ascension of our Lord Jesu Christ went up unto heaven, and like as he had been asleep without any sign or token of whatsoever dolour he took the right bencurous rest of death.

And who that could recount all the miracles done by him, howbeit that to none ne is possible but alone to him which can number or tell the multitude of stars, and imposeth to each one their names, but because that, to one right great inconvenience and dishonour were, if by sloth he refrained himself from uttering, and kept still such things that are and appertain to the praising and laud of our Lord, and namely thereas plenty and abundance of his praising is or should be, that the said miracles are infinite or without end, nevertheless we shall rehearse some of them.

Then as it is recorded in the book long since made and accomplished of his life and of his virtues, that at his invocation by vows and prayers, by some devoutly made unto God, and to the Saint in divers places were fourteen dead raised, reckoned always in the said number two children living within their mother's womb and dead before their baptism which sithe received life.[8] And at the invocation of the said S. Ives ten demoniacs, mad folk, or filled with wicked spirits, were delivered from their forsenery or madness, and from all wicked spirits. Thirteen contracts, or filled with paralysis, were by the same restored in good health. Three blind were by him illumined. Divers folk, in ten places, all with their goods were kept and saved from drowning in the sea. One perfectly hydropic or filled with dropsy was entirely cured. Another that had the stone great as an egg, and the genitors as great as a man's head, was restituted unto health.

One condemned to be hanged fell three times from the gallows, and all whole was delivered and let go. A woman to whom the milk wanted within her paps were filled full of it. Things lost by divers persons and in divers places were found and recovered by miracles. Two dumb childien and divers others that had lost the use of the tongue were restituted of their speaking. Three or four women, with all their birth, were delivered from the peril of death. The fire taken in three divers places was quenched and put out, and both men, women, and children, and goods kept from burning without to be hurted, ne in no manner of wise damaged. A woman sore aggrieved with an axes[9] took a little bread that before had been wet in water by the hands of the saint, ate it and recovered health.

---

[8] Some of the items mentioned in this and the sentences that follow and in the next paragraph have been reworded within the main text: see *Chapter 5*.

[9] 'Axe' or 'axes' appears to mean ague or agues (pain or pains). The word occurs again in relation to the death and resurrection of the Archbishop of Narbonne, who had been vexed by strong axes (again see *Chapter 5*).

The saint himself giving foison alms, the corn multiplied in his garret, and the bread in his hand sometimes. Many sick folk were healed of divers sicknesses and dolours only to have touched his hood. A man dressing the wheel of his water-mill, on whom suddenly the water came from high rushing, and he besought the holy S. Ives, and anon he was saved from drowning. On a time, as the said saint said mass, while he celebrated and held up the body of our Lord, a great resplendor appeared about it, which soon after the elevation was done, disappeared and vanished away. A post ordained to the work or making of a bridge, not convenable to the said work for fault of half a foot of length, after the prayer of the carpenters done unto the saint, was the said post found long enough and convenable to the foresaid work. In time of a great inundation or flowing, which covered the ways and places, the sign of the cross made with the said holy man's hand on the water it ceased and ebbed away.

The hood which he gave to a poor man, as above is said, and went barehead homeward, God that had himself in form or likeness of a poor man received the said hood, as it may be believed, sent to him again the said hood, whereof was great and marvellous miracle. On a time when he had given all his bread to poor folks, loaves of bread were brought to him enough to suffice him and the poor people in his fellowship withal, by a woman unknown, the which after her present delivered, vanished away and never was seen after. On another time, as he had received a poor man appearing right foul and disformed, and over foul in clothing, and had made him to eat and set hand at his own dish with him, this poor man departing and saying: God be with you and at your help, his gown that before was wonder foul, as it is said became so white, and of so great resplendor and shining, and his face so fair appeared and so bright, that all the house was replenished and filled with great light.

The archbishop of Narbonne was vexed with a strong axes, and by the feebleness of his nature was reputed and holden as for dead of all them which about him were, for his eyes were shut in manner of a dead man. At the invocation or calling to S. Ives made for the salue of the said archbishop by his parents and friends, with weepings, vows, devotions, was the foresaid archbishop through the merits of the saint restored unto life, sight and good health, by the grace and virtue of him of whom it is written that he enlumineth the eyes, giveth life, health and blessing, light, sapience, the which God, creator, enluminator, and saviour be thanked, praised and worshipped by all the siecle and siecles.

Index

abandoned people 67
advocate 47 67
alcohol 67
Aquinas, St Thomas 30
arbitrator 68
Aristotle 31
asceticism 56
austerity 29

bailiffs 67
barristers 67
basket justice 51
Belle Isle 26
Bernadette of Lourdes 25
Betjeman, Sir John 76
bias 51
biblical aspects 56
bigotry 19
Bishops Palace 33
Black and White Flag 26
blasphemies 67
blessings 52
blind people given sight 56
Bonnets Rouges 26
bribes/bribery 19 20 51 68
Britanny, patron saint 67

Cambridgeshire 76
career 29
cathedral 15 21 29 66
champion of the poor 15 19 37 58 64 67
charity 68
Clement VI (Pope Clement) 57

common touch 30
concise approach 49
confessional booths 41
conflict/conflict resolution 19
Cornwall 76
cooking smells, stealing 21
corruption 19 20 68
counsel/counselling 47
Court of Appeal 22
crime 19
Criminal Cases Review Commission 22
crusades 30
cures 52

death 50
defender of the poor, see *champion of the poor*
discrimination 19
Dominicans 31
down-and-out 41
drowning, saving from 56 57
dumb people made to speak 56

early life 29
écoute, ding, dong ... 43
education 30 *et seq.* 37
enquiry, see *Papal Enquiry*

fairness 16 19
fasting 30 67
Franciscans/Franciscan order 31 67
French Revolution 15 29
'Friend of the Poor', see *champion of the poor*

Genesius (St Genesius) 23
'going to St Yves' 65 76 ghosts 25
Golden Legend, see under *legend*
Gothic 20 54 63
Guincamp 67
hair-shirt 67
Hardy, Thomas 76
healing, see *sick people/healing*
Helouri, Erwan (Yves Helouri)
   (some main entries) 15 19 20 26
   29 37 55 *et seq*
Holy Grail 25
honest lawyer 68
hospital (foundation of free
   hospital) 29 38
human rights 15

Ia, St (St Ives) 75 76
intolerance, see *tolerance/intolerance*
Ivo, St (St Ives) 76

Jehan 30 32
Jessie James 15
Jesus Christ 55
Joan of Arc 25
judge 32 33 47 49 67
justice 16 19 67
Justice of the Peace 15 20

Kelly, Ned 19
Kermartin 20f 29

lame people, paralysis, etc 38 55
land of beef 69
Lannion 20 64
La Vie de Jésus 70

law/lawyers/patron saint of
   lawyers 15 32 33 47 67
Lee, John 56
legal aid 51
legend of St Yves 19 *et seq.* 41
   Golden Legend (The Golden
   Legend) 56 77
Louvannec 51 68

mediation/mediator 16 47
Merlin 25
Minihy-Tréguier 20 29
miracle/miracles 15 48 55 *et seq.*
misfit 16 37
More, Thomas 23
myths 21 25

Narbonne, Archbisop of 57
notaries 67

open door policy 29 38
Orléans 32
orphans 38 67
outsider/outsiders 16 37 38

Paimpol 20
Papal Enquiry 21 26 29 38 47 48 55
Pardon of St Yves 25 64
Paris/University of Paris 30 32
Place du Martray 41 74
poor/poverty 15 19 30 37 38 47 57
   65
   poor box 16 37
   poor persons' advocate, etc. 37 47
   and see *champion of the poor; rich
   and poor*
Pope Clement VI 58

preacher/preaching 55 56
prejudice 19
Pretty Boy Floyd 15
priest 51 67
prison 67
privilege 29
pro bono 51
Protestant Britain 15
punishment 19

Quimper 26

radical/radicalism 23
Ramsey Abbey 76 78
relics/reliquary 65
remembrance 20
Renan, Ernest 69-70
Rennes 33 49
restorative justice 68
revolution, see *French Revolution*
rich and poor 41 43 46
Robin Hood 15 16
Roman Catholic/Roman Catholicism 15
Romanesque tower 63
Round Table 25

saints 21 *et seq*
sardine 28
separatism 26
shaming 20
shelter 29
sick people/healing 38 56 57
sleep, going without 39 67
'small money' 40 41
Soloman, King 73
St Enodoc 76

superstition 25
symbolism 68

taxation, campaigns against 68
Thomas Aquinas (St Thomas) 30
tomb 64
Tredez 51 68
tributes 16 58 63 *et seq.*
Tugdall (St Tugdall or 'Tudwall') 16 63 70

underdog 20
underground (French wartime underground) 26

vagabonds 37 38 67
Vatican, The 16 26
vision 55

Winchester 38
wisdom/popular wisdom 22 49
witness/witnesses 26 29 38 55

Yves (St Yves)
  legend 19 25
  Pardon of St Yves, see that entry
  St Yves' tomb 16
  see also *Helouri, Erwan*

Key Works on Penal Reform

Restoring Respect for Justice
A Symposium
~ Martin Wright
With a new Foreword by Howard Zehr

This **enhanced** Waterside Press Classic records a symposium at which imaginary presenters - a Politician, Judge, Psychologist, Probation Officer, Victim Assistance Worker, Philosopher and Mediator discuss crime and punishment. This is the springboard for **Martin Wright**'s review of developments in the field of Restorative Justice, where he is highly regarded as a commentator and authority, having been director of the Howard League for Penal Reform, policy officer of Victim Support and librarian at the Cambridge Institute of Criminology.

Restoring Respect for Justice challenges many 'sacred cows' of crime and punishment by focusing on the effect on the people who suffer directly, the victims. A key theme is that if society as a whole does not encourage respect then it ought to be no surprise if offenders have scant regard for the property, physical integrity or rights of others. A bad system can itself serve to weaken rather than improve safety and security.

Universally acclaimed since it was first issued in 1999 and essential reading for practitioners and students alike, this enhanced edition of *Restoring Respect for Justice* points to the dangers of a punitive mind-set and reflects on the arguments and data in favour of an effective, inclusionary, community-based response to crime.

2nd Edition | 250 pages | February 2008 | ISBN 978-1-904380-38-2

Opening Up a Closed World...

Full catalogue includes Prisons, Policing, Criminal Justice, Restorative Justice, History, Biography, Policy, Youth Crime, Drugs, Women, Crime and Punishment and much more - please visit our website.

www.WatersidePress.co.uk

≋ WATERSIDE PRESS

Key Works on Penal Reform

MAKING GOOD
Prisons, Punishment and Beyond
~ Martin Wright

Now reprinted with additional material by the author, and a new Foreword by one of the UK's leading penal reformers, **Baroness Vivien Stern**.

A classic and original work in the vanguard of Restorative Justice. The author argues that the real need is for fundamental rethinking, rather than short-term tinkering with a prison system in an intolerable state of crisis.

Martin Wright demonstrates that neither the conservative idea of deterrence through punishment nor the liberal ideal of rehabilitation has worked. In their place he proposes the basis for a radical but carefully worked out practical philosophy which places the emphasis on the offender making amends to the victim, and to society as a whole for the damage caused.

2nd Edition | 330 pages | February 2008 | ISBN 978-1-904380-41-2

Doing Justice Better
The Politics of Restorative Justice ~ David J Cornwell

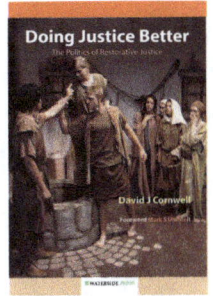

An **uncompromising appraisal** of the unique penal crisis affecting Britain and other Western-style democracies. Escalating resort to prisons, longer sentences, overcrowded and ineffective regimes, high rates of re-offending and eclectic penal policy all combine to fuel this crisis, whilst failing to reduce offending. In *Doing Justice Better*, **David J Cornwell** argues that the symptoms of this penal malaise are grounded in media sensationalism of crime and the need of politicians (and their advisers) to retain electoral credibility. Change is long overdue, but it requires a fresh, **contemporary penology** based on Restorative Justice. The book challenges the status quo, asks 'different questions' and places victims of crime at the centre of the criminal justice process.

August 2007 | 200 pages | ISBN 978-1-904380-34-4

WATERSIDE PRESS

www.ingramcontent.com/pod-product-compliance
Lightning Source LLC
LaVergne TN
LVHW021117080426
835512LV00011B/2557